S0-ADC-934

THE HOWARD BROS.
CIRCUS
—❧ MODEL ❧—

The John and Mable Ringling Museum of Art
Sarasota, Florida

Printing by Serbin Print Marketing & Publishing
Sarasota, Florida
Robin K. Clark, Project Director
Judy Webster and Anne Christensen,
Serbin Designers
Katie Booth and Libby Bennett,
Ringling Designers

Copyright 2016 © The John and Mable
Ringling Museum of Art
The State Art Museum of Florida
5401 Bay Shore Road
Sarasota, Florida 34243
www.ringling.org

Second Edition

All rights reserved. No part of this publication
may be reproduced, stored in a retrieval system,
or transmitted in any form or by any means,
electronic, mechanical, recording or otherwise,
without prior permission, in writing, from The
John and Mable Ringling Museum of Art.

ISBN: 9780916758295
LCCN: 2016950311

TheRingling

THE JOHN & MABLE RINGLING MUSEUM OF ART
STATE ART MUSEUM OF FLORIDA | FLORIDA STATE UNIVERSITY

TABLE OF CONTENTS

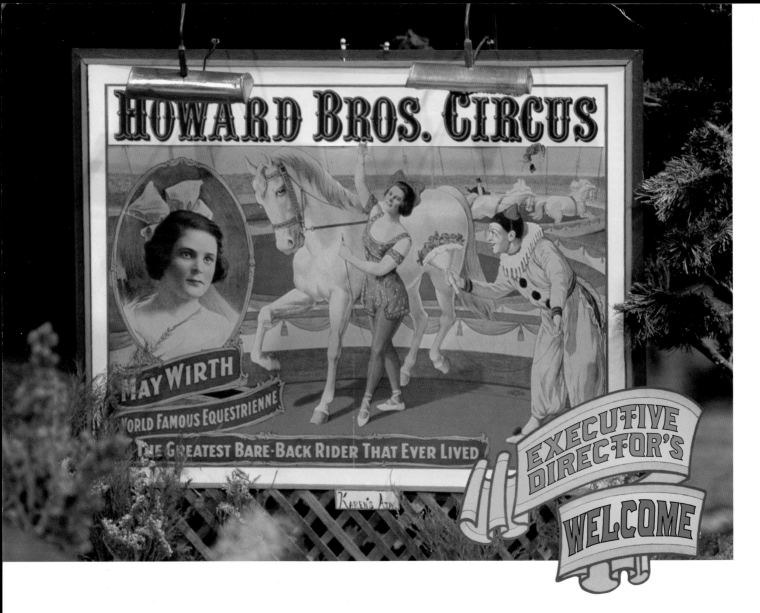

It has been ten years since the Howard Bros. Circus Model was installed at The John and Mable Ringling Museum of Art. During that time over 2.9 million ladies, gentleman and children of all ages have been captivated by Howard Tibbals' more than 42,000 piece replica that is the largest miniature circus model in the world.

Howard became fascinated with the circus as a young child when he spent summers with his grandparents in Fairmont, West Virginia which was annually visited by circuses. Howard was intrigued with how the circus worked, how all the parts operating together created a magnificent spectacle like no other. He began building models of circus wagons at seven-years-old and hasn't stopped since. For 60 years Howard has been working on this astounding replica and continues to add new pieces. Accurate in every detail, the model is based on his

extensive collection of vintage photographs, numbering in the hundreds of thousands, supplemented by historic posters, heralds, programs, route cards, and oral histories.

Spending part of the year at his home in Knoxville, Tennessee, and the remainder in Sarasota, Florida, Howard maintains a workshop in both homes where he continues to work on the model at least thirty hours a week. The Howard Bros. Circus Model is a marvel and a testament to one man's passion for a great American tradition and entertainment enterprise – the traveling circus.

The model captures a time when the tented circus was at its largest. Packing up and moving nearly every single day during a nine month tour, the circus was the epitome of logistical engineering. Every detail was thought out and every action was at its most efficient. Over 1,300 circus personnel and 900 animals, along with the canvas and hardware to construct the big top and multiple support tents had to be picked up and moved to the next venue, several hundred miles away, in time for the next performance. The circus brought thrilling acts, talented performers and exotic animals from all over the world to large cities and small towns across America.

Steven High
Executive Director

ACKNOWLEDGEMENTS

Special thanks to Howard and Janice Tibbals for their generosity and dedication and to former Florida State University president Talbot "Sandy" D'Alemberte, who worked directly with Howard to bring the Howard Bros. Circus Model to The Ringling. Gratitude also goes to John Thrasher, President of Florida State University, Sally E. McRorie, Provost, and Peter Weisher, Dean of the College of Fine Arts, for their support of The Ringling, the Tibbals' endeavors, and circus projects. Deep appreciation is extended also to the staff and volunteers, who assisted with the installation and continue to work with Howard Tibbals on the model to make it the most accurate replica of the great American circus under canvas.

t the turn of the 20th century, the arrival of the circus was an anticipated, longed for event all across America. Weeks before the arrival of the show, excitement was fueled by the bombastic posters announcing an all-new enormous show "loaded with ten thousand wonders from every land" would shortly arrive. While today we are surrounded by all types of advertisements, circus owners faced a very different situation. They had the formidable task of promoting a one-day event without the aid of television, radio or the Internet. Their basic marketing tool was the circus poster. Printed by the thousands, the colorful

lithographs were plastered on every available space, filled up every available shop window, and often covered entire sides of buildings, making sure that no one could overlook the upcoming arrival of the greatest circus ever.

When the long awaited circus arrived, the day was filled with amazing and wonderful events. Those rising early could watch as the enormous circus train pulled into town. Animals from all over the world and hundreds of parade and baggage wagons were unloaded and taken to the circus lot. In the early hours of the morning, an empty town lot teemed with a thousand workers hammering in stakes, lacing canvas, raising tent tops, cooking breakfast, and grooming animals. Within a span of a few hours, the once deserted field was transformed into a magical, colossal canvas city. The free, miles-long street parade followed, complete with band wagons, beautiful ladies on horse back, clowns, cage wagons with roaring lions, elephants, and gilded chariots that wound their way through the town

drawing people to the streets and roof tops. Shops closed and schools canceled classes. Towns all over the country were for a single magical day transformed. The circus was also a source of information and culture. It brought the world to America's doorstep by introducing electricity, movies, the automobile as well as foreign cultures and people to the American public.

As many as 13,000 people could enjoy a single performance under the colossal canvas big top. The circus traveled with over 1,300 people, hundreds of animals and everything needed to put on the show. Over the course of a season, the circus would travel up to 20,000 miles and perform in 150 towns and cities. In no more than twenty cities did the circus perform for more than one day. No wonder that armies looked closely at the logistics of the circus!

The circus day ended with the final act in the big top and, reluctantly, the town returned to normal with only wonderful memories as the circus train headed off into the night.

Captured by the magic of the circus and the astounding process of moving it from town to town, Howard Tibbals wanted to create his own model circus. For over sixty years, he has worked to produce the most accurate representation of the American circus when it was at it largest under canvas. Every detail of the circus lot has been recreated exactly as it would have been on the sixteen to twenty acre circus lot, from the parade wagon heading down Main Street, the ticket seller making exact change, and the menagerie filled with exotic animals from all over the world, to the big top filled with peerless performers, both human and animal.

Ladies and gentlemen, boys and girls, children of all ages, the circus has arrived, so step right up and tour the incredible Howard Bros. Circus Model, the world's largest miniature circus.

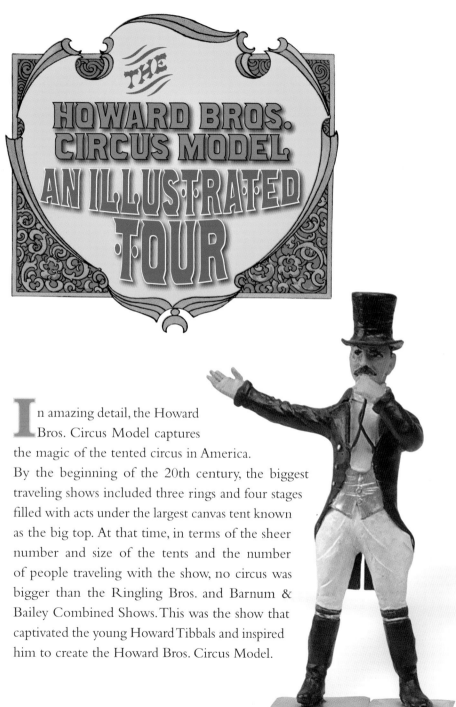

THE HOWARD BROS. CIRCUS MODEL AN ILLUSTRATED TOUR

Howard Tibbals in the big top of the Howard Bros. Circus Model.

In amazing detail, the Howard Bros. Circus Model captures the magic of the tented circus in America. By the beginning of the 20th century, the biggest traveling shows included three rings and four stages filled with acts under the largest canvas tent known as the big top. At that time, in terms of the sheer number and size of the tents and the number of people traveling with the show, no circus was bigger than the Ringling Bros. and Barnum & Bailey Combined Shows. This was the show that captivated the young Howard Tibbals and inspired him to create the Howard Bros. Circus Model.

The circus day began before most people got out of bed. By 3 a.m. the first of the four sections of the massive circus train arrived in town. Called the flying squadron, this section carried the equipment and crew to lay out the circus lot and to set up the draft horse, cookhouse and dining tents. The second section of the train carried the canvas and poles for the rest of the tents, including the big top and seating. The concession wagons for the midway, wardrobe, and props to be placed inside of the tents arrived on the third section.

After the lot was prepared and the tents raised, the final section of the train brought the performers, horses and elephants to town. Within a few hours of their arrival, doors opened for the day's first performance. In 1928, the Ringling show traveled on forty-six flat cars, twenty-eight stock cars, twenty-four coaches, including dining cars and John Ringling's private car, and the two advertising cars—one hundred railcars in all!

The big top was not the only place to see death defying feats of extraordinary skill and bravery. Unloading the wagons from the circus train was a major production, requiring coordinated teamwork. The train crew was responsible for moving wagons that weighed as much as six tons each.

Once the inclined runs were placed at the end of the cars, a pair of horses pulled the wagon down the flat car. One of the crew steered a wagon tongue to keep the front wheels of the wagon traveling straight.

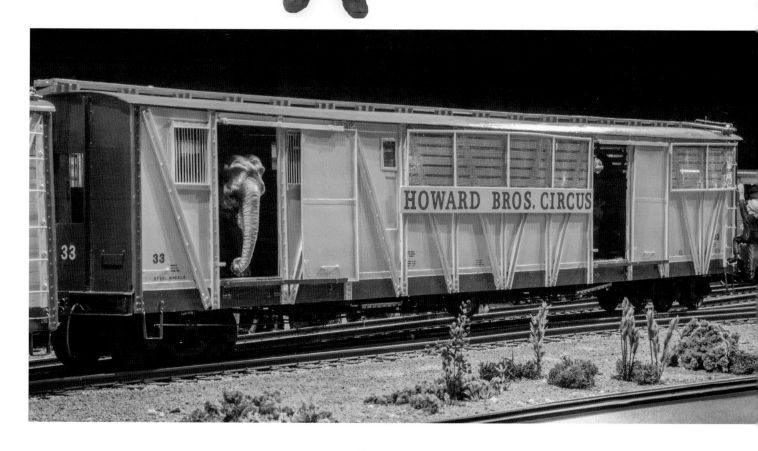

Lowering the wagon down the inclined run was the most dangerous part of the process. If the wagon rolled too quickly, the crew could lose control. To prevent such accidents, a man known as the "snubber" controlled the wagon's speed down the runs by a system of ropes and capstans. Once off the train, the wagon was hitched to a new team of horses and pulled to the lot. During the period between 1919 and 1938, the Ringling show unloaded as many as 150 wagons at each stop.

The model railroad layout has:

- 59 railroad cars
- 850 feet of custom designed ¾-inch scale rail
- 7,500 six-inch wooden cross ties
- 11,000 rail plates
- 32,000 metal half-inch spikes
- 800 pounds of gravel

COOKHOUSE

The cookhouse was the very first tent set up on the circus lot. Before sunrise workers had the tent erected and breakfast cooking.

Soon the air was filled with the aroma of hot cakes, sausages and eggs. The cookhouse prepared three meals a day for more than 1,300 workers and performers.

Provisions needed daily:

- 2 barrels of sugar
- 30 gallons of milk
- 36 bags of table salt
- 50 bushels of potatoes
- 110 dozen oranges
- 200 pounds of coffee and tea
- 226 dozen eggs
- 285 pounds of butter
- 350 pounds of salad
- 1,300 pounds of fresh vegetables
- 2,220 loaves of bread
- 2,470 pounds of fresh meat
- 3,600 ears of corn

DINING TENT

The hotel flag was raised over the dining tent to signal to the workers, staff and performers that it was mealtime. Each person with the circus had a designated seat at a table set with porcelain-covered steel plates, silverware, a water pitcher, condiments, bread, and butter. To feed all of the personnel breakfast, lunch, and dinner, the waiters would serve over 3,900 meals daily.

The model dining tent has:

- 53 pickle jars
- 140 ketchup bottles
- 144 bottles of Worcestershire sauce
- 145 sugar bowls
- 145 salt shakers
- 200 hamburger buns with lettuce

Circus Lingo

- **High school horses:** Horses that perform a dressage act, completing choreographed moves without seeming to be commanded.
- **Liberty act:** Horses that are trained to perform without riders or reins.
- **Pad room:** Tent used for the performing horses (term coming from the blankets used by riding acts).
- **Ring stock:** Any animal that performs in the circus.
- **Rosinbacks:** Horses used by bareback riders. Rosin powder is applied to the horse's back to make the rider's footing more secure.

RING STOCK TENT

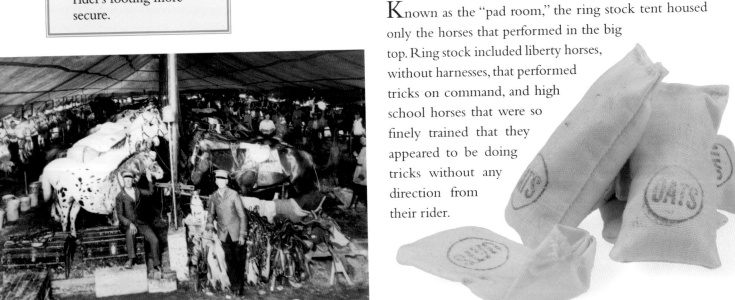

Known as the "pad room," the ring stock tent housed only the horses that performed in the big top. Ring stock included liberty horses, without harnesses, that performed tricks on command, and high school horses that were so finely trained that they appeared to be doing tricks without any direction from their rider.

Why is John Ringling on the lot?

The youngest of the five founding brothers can be seen receiving mail in the backyard of the Howard Bros. Circus Model. Although Howard Tibbals gave his name to his miniature circus, the entire show is based on the Ringling Bros. and Barnum & Bailey circus of the early 20th century. When asked, Howard Tibbals smiles and says that John Ringling is checking out the competition.

BACKYARD

The backyard was the area where the performers, staff and workers spent their time between performances. Hidden from the general public behind the tented city, the backyard was filled with the activities of workers preparing equipment and performers preparing for the show.

Elaborate floats and fantastically costumed animals and performers lined up in the backyard to enter the big top for the spectacle display. Usually the opening feature of a show, the "spec," included as many people and animals as the director of the show could costume, all parading around the track in the big top. The beautiful wardrobe, exotic characters, and incredible floats hinted at the excitement to come in the performances.

REST TENT

Various rest tents were set up in the backyard for circus personnel. The band, with over thirty members, shared a rest tent with the fifty or more ushers that worked in the big top. There were other rest tents where workers slept between setting up the lot in the early hours of the morning and tearing it down after the last show of the night.

Ringling Brothers and Barnum & Bailey's
Concert Band
1933

MERLE EVANS
Bandmaster
1918 - - 1933

INDORSING CONN INSTRUMENTS *and* LEEDY DRUMS

The Howard Bros.
Circus Model has:

- 39 band members
- 29 ushers
- 5 tubas
- 11 trumpets
- 3 drums
- 10 saxophones
- 7 clarinets
- 1 banjo

PERFORMERS' ENTRANCE

When it was show time, performers entered the big top through the backside opening known as the performers' entrance or back door. Every act and display waited immediately outside of the tent until their entry was cued by the music coming from the big top. Just outside of the entrance was "clown alley," where the clowns stored all of their props and gags.

Clowns abound at the circus

There are 67 clowns on the Howard Bros. Circus lot. They include:

Whiteface clowns with all white faces and features, like the nose, mouth and eyebrows, painted on in black or red.

Auguste clowns with a dark flesh tone as the underpaint and exaggerated facial features painted in red, white and black.

Character clowns made up as exaggerated versions of a normal human face. One type of character clown is the hobo.

PERFORMERS' DRESSING TENT

Before the performers arrived in town the dressing tent was raised and each performer's trunk was placed in position, along with two pails of water. The small trunks contained everything

that a performer needed to prepare for their act except for special wardrobe and props. The tent was divided by two canvas walls, with one side for men, one for women and the center for the wardrobe wagon.

The model's dressing tent is furnished with:

- 104 trunks
- 99 water buckets
- 61 bottles of nail polish
- 46 bottles of perfume
- 73 sticks of make-up
- 89 jars of make-up
- 41 rolls of toilet paper
- 46 combs
- 180 mirrors
- 66 boxes of tissue

PRIVATE TENTS

Some of the most famous center ring stars required their own private tents in the backyard. The tent and a private room on the circus train were generally written into their annual contract. These featured performers furnished their tents with all of the comforts of home including comfortable chairs, pillows, throw blankets, oriental rugs and pets. Some even had portable wooden floors.

Lillian Leitzel

Learning about circus life

In order to make the model historically accurate, Howard Tibbals thoroughly researched every aspect of circus life. During his interview of equestrian artist May Wirth, he learned that her most vivid memories of the backyard were of washing her hair in a bucket and of the parrot that sat on a perch in her private tent.

May Wirth

GOLIATH

One of the favorite attractions of the circus in the early 20th century was Goliath. Weighing three and a quarter tons, the giant sea elephant traveled in a specially constructed water tank on the train. When he was not being wheeled around the big top's track on a wagon, he was housed in a tank inside his own tent and was fed 150 pounds of fish per day.

MIDWAY

A visitor's first circus experience was on the midway. The circus lot came alive with the sights, sounds, and smells. There were concessionaires hawking their goods, ticket sellers crying "Step Right Up," and the calliope whistling away at the entrance to the side show. The brightly colored wagons and the strange images on the side show banners all added to the excitement.

HOWARD BROS.
CIRCUS
SIDE SHOWS
CONTINUOUS PERFORMANCE
SKEETS
HUMAN
SIDE SHO
25¢

Circus Lingo

- **Grease joint:** Grill concession wagon that cooked hot dogs and hamburgers.
- **Midway:** Area between the lot entrance and the marquee where the concessions and side show tent were located.
- **Pitchmen:** Employees selling concessions on the midway.
- **Red Wagon:** Main office and ticket wagon of the show.
- **Rubbermen or bag men:** Balloon vendors.
- **Talker:** Person making the outside spiel for a side show attraction—never called "barker."

SIDE SHOW

The side show, which was sometimes called the "kid show," was the smallest of the three tents that visitors could enter. Entry into the side show required a separate admission ticket from the rest of the circus experience. Men sold tickets from stands in front of the side show's entrance shouting the "ballyhoo" that described the strange and marvelous sights to be seen for just a few cents.

The side show bannerline, composed of brightly painted images of human curiosities, lined the midway in front of the side show tent. These exciting and exotic images of the Human Pin Cushion, the Fire Proof Man and the Tiny Town performers hinted at the wonders housed in the side show. Sometimes a few dancers or even a sword swallower performed on the stage in front to attract customers.

Daisy Doll and Clyde Ingalls

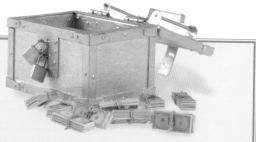

What no one can see

Although unseen by visitors, the commissary wagon and each of the three ticket wagons are as detailed inside as on the outside. Functional drawers and cabinets, furnishing such as chairs, desks and sinks and other details reflect the remarkable accuracy of the model.

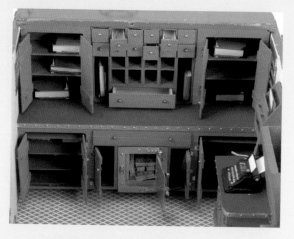

TICKET WAGONS

Opposite the side show bannerline, three brightly painted ticket wagons were prominently placed along the midway. Lines formed from the open windows at each wagon as visitors purchased general admission or reserved seats for that day's circus performance.

MAIN ENTRANCE

From the front lot, visitors made their way to the main entrance. Here the mass of people funneled through five gates. Although the marquee advertised the entrance to the show, visitors actually found themselves entering the menagerie tent.

Most of the wild animals on display in the menagerie were kept in beautifully carved and painted cage wagons. Like the calliope on the midway, these wagons were examples of the art of woodcarving. All the decorative figures and scrollwork were carved by hand and attached to the wagon. All the cage wagons had panels that could be placed over the bars to enclose and protect the animals during travel.

Included in the 925 animals seen at the Howard Bros. Circus Model are:

- Horses
- Elephants
- Baboons
- Parrots
- Armadillos
- Bears
- Seals
- Pigeons
- Musk oxen
- Llamas
- Emus
- Goats
- Gaurs
- Camels
- Bison
- Zebras

For many Americans, the circus was the first place they saw animals from other continents. Along with the expected elephants, lions and zebras, visitors found hippopotami, giraffes, and even polar bears! Other exotic animals that might be seen in the menagerie included orangutans, macaws and kangaroos.

BIG TOP

Fittingly, the performance tent, the largest of all the tents on the lot, was commonly referred to as the big top. The raising of the tent was an amazing act of skill, coordination and practice. In less than four hours, the six center poles, seventy-four quarter poles, 122 sidewall poles, 550 stakes and 26,000 yards of canvas became the big top, the centerpiece of the circus lot.

Lou Jacobs

Seating in the big top could accommodate as many as 13,000 people. The folding chairs along the length of the tent were reserved seats and were more expensive than the general admission bleacher seats located along the curved ends of the tent. If all the seats were sold, straw bales were placed in front of the stands to provide extra seating for children. This packed big top was known as a "straw house."

Unus

Performances inside the big top were an astounding sight. At any given moment, action could be taking place in the three rings, on the four stages, around the hippodrome track, or in the air above the rings. In 1926, each performance lasted about two and a half hours, without intermission, and included more than 800 artists performing in twenty-two displays.

 ## DOG WAGONS

Performing dogs were often strays or purchased from
the local pound, because these mixed breed dogs were
usually very intelligent and learned tricks quickly. The
dogs traveled in special accommodations. Wagons 98
and 99 were designed specifically for the dogs, with each
animal having its own space in the wagon. In between
performances the dogs were kept in outdoor kennels.

🎪 DRAFT HORSE TENTS 🎪

Along with the performing horses, the circus carried over 400 draft horses, known as baggage stock, kept in two large tents in the back lot when not working. These strong horses pulled wagons and even helped raise the poles and canvas for the tents. After the lot was set up, the draft horses rested in their tents. The attendants removed the harnesses, groomed, and fed the horses before putting them back to work in the evening to tear down the show.

🏷 BLACKSMITH SHOP 🏷

The blacksmith department carried the equipment needed to keep the show moving. Forges and anvils were set up at each lot to allow the blacksmith to repair wagon parts and shoe horses. There was also a leather worker who cared for all of the animal harnesses.

Circus Lingo

- **Boss canvasman:** Person in charge of putting up and taking down the tents on the circus lot.
- **Boss hostler:** Person in charge of all the baggage horses.
- **Lot man:** Supervisor who locates the various tents on the show grounds for each stand.
- **Razorbacks:** Workers who load and unload the circus railroad cars.
- **Roustabout:** Circus worker or laborer.
- **Sledge gang:** The crew who pound in tent stakes.

Howard Tibbals
on the circus lot.

MASTER MODEL BUILDER
HOWARD TIBBALS

My fascination with the circus began about fifty-five years ago. After the show, other children dreamed and had fond memories of the circus. But that night never ended for me. I continued to watch way past my bedtime as the great circus folded up and packed away, was loaded onto the railroad train and departed into the night for another town.

— Howard Tibbals, 2000

Howard Tibbals wants everyone to know about the marvels of the tented circus, its impact on towns across America, and its influence on the history of entertainment and advertising. To accomplish this, he has spent over sixty years building a ¾-inch (one-sixteenth life size) scale replica of the Ringling Bros. and Barnum & Bailey Combined Shows from 1919 through 1950s.

Born in Logan, West Virginia, Howard Tibbals was taken to his first circus at the age of three in Pittsburgh, Pennsylvania. He remembers nothing of that first encounter with the circus, but he does remember clearly the next circus he saw in 1941, right down to the bale of hay that he sat on to see the show.

During World War II, Howard Tibbals spent summers with his grandparents in Fairmont, West Virginia, where circuses annually performed. Through binoculars, he examined the equipment unloaded from the wagons and observed how the tents were set up. By the time he was seven years old, he was creating his own circus by converting toy trucks into circus vehicles, making tents out of scraps of cloth, and building his own circus wagons. As a teenager, he read "Hand Carved Circus" by Rod van Every in the February 1948 *Popular Mechanics* magazine. The article outlined the logistics of the Ringling show and the layout of the big top. Tibbals was captivated and dreamed

of creating a miniature circus. In 1956, while a student at North Carolina State University, he started working on the six-pole big top tent. Using a Sears Kenmore sewing machine, he cut out and stitched together thirty-five yards of unbleached muslin to create the big top.

After graduating from college, Tibbals returned to his hometown and joined the family's flooring company, but his dream of building the most accurate circus model continued. He seized every opportunity to visit circus lots, to measure wagons, and to talk with performers and workers. Quickly, Howard Tibbals realized that carving animals and sculpting people for his colossal canvas city would far exceed one lifetime, so he tapped the abilities of others to carve and sculpt. In 1965, Tibbals exhibited the incredible Howard Bros. Circus Model for the first time. From 1965 through 2005, over 3.1 million people saw the model in ten venues.

How long did it take to create the big top of the Howard Bros. Circus?
18 years! He worked on the big top from 1956 to 1974.

Which wagon did Howard Tibbals build first?
Wagon No. 40, which was completed in 1959 – the first of 154 wagons.

How long did it take Howard Tibbals to build a model circus wagon?
Most of the baggage wagons took 60 to 70 hours; however, the more elaborate parade wagons took up to 700 hours to build.

After so many years working on the model, Tibbals wanted a permanent home for the circus model. After research, Howard Tibbals chose the John and Mable Ringling Museum of Art. When finally installed in the Circus Museum's Tibbals Learning Center, Tibbals had the opportunity to see his model as he has so long envisioned it. Janice Tibbals, his wife, said, "I am so pleased for him, because this circus has been his life's work." For both Howard and Janice, it is wonderful to be able to share his model with museum visitors. Even though his model has found a permanent home, Howard Tibbals still sees that there is work to do. "The model isn't totally built yet," he said, "the circus train needs 85 railroad cars. There's still a lot I want to add."

The Model Builder's Mentor: Harold Dunn

In 1958 while in college in North Carolina, Howard Tibbals met Harold Dunn, a circus model builder, and saw the Dunn Circus Model on exhibit at a department store. Tibbals enthusiastically questioned Dunn about his model and the circus. Dunn was impressed with Tibbals' interest and the two became friends. In 1982 at the World's Fair in Knoxville, Tennessee, the two men collaborated to create a 6,500 square foot circus exhibition, which included both the Howard Bros. Circus Model and the Dunn Bros. Circus Model.

Born in 1908 in Jet, Oklahoma, Harold Dunn grew up during the heyday of the American tented circus. As the oldest child, he learned woodcarving from his grandfather. After seeing a circus at the age of five, Dunn became enamored with its excitement and wonder. In 1938, he began work on his ½-inch to the foot miniature circus, which he first exhibited in 1946. The exhibit was such a success that he decided to turn his hobby into a career. For over thirty years, Dunn and his wife Barbara exhibited the Dunn Bros. Circus Model in hundreds of department stores across America, drawing huge crowds.

In 2005, with the assistance of Harold Dunn's son Kenneth, the parade and spectacle pieces of the Dunn Bros. Circus Model found a permanent home at the Circus Museum's Tibbals Learning Center. The one hundred and forty-eight linear feet exhibit features a street parade of elaborately carved wagons, as well as fanciful floats of the circus spectacle.

– *Melissa Porreca McCarriagher*

Howard Tibbals
unloading the
model circus.

INSTALLATION OF THE WORLD'S LARGEST CIRCUS MODEL

The same amazing precision used to move the real circus was employed to install the Howard Bros. Circus Model at The John and Mable Ringling Museum of Art. For fourteen months, Howard Tibbals, his wife Janice, a team of wonderful volunteers, skilled artists, and talented staff, worked to place the Howard Bros. Circus Model in the specially built 10,000 square foot gallery in the Circus Museum's Tibbals Learning Center.

Sarasota artist, Pam Marwede, took three months to paint the sky and clouds on the 6,500 square feet of walls and ceiling above the model. Scale model builders, SMARTT of Miami, created the Knoxville, Tennessee, skyline working from a replica created by David Duncan, a Knoxville resident and railroad historian.

Seven months of the installation focused on the construction of the train yard, trestle bridge, and passenger terminal. Volunteers hammered in each of the 32,000 metal spikes. Once the rail yard was completed, the Howard Bros. Circus could finally roll into town. Just like the real circus, the wagons on the 59-railroad cars housed all the tents, poles, stakes, and equipment. While the circus would take six hours to prepare the lot for the

Working on the railroad

Over 850 feet of custom-designed ¾-inch scale rail was laid by volunteers to create ten parallel siding lines, which required 7,500 six-inch wooden crossties, 11,000 rail plates, and approximately 32,000 metal spikes (one half inch in length). The train yard used 800 pounds of gravel to duplicate the rail lines around Knoxville.

Just like the real show

When the Howard Bros. Circus Model arrived at The Ringling all of its equipment was loaded in the circus wagons, which were each placed on the flat cars in the railroad yard. Just like the real show, the model was set up tent by tent.

performance, it took six months to complete the set up for the circus model. The Howard Bros. Circus Model was unloaded in the same order as its colossal counterpart. As each wagon was moved off the train and before any of the equipment was placed on the circus lot, each unique piece of the circus – from the 950-square foot big top tent right down to the tissue boxes, forks, and lipstick tubes – was photographed and catalogued.

First off the train and onto the circus lot was the model's dining tent. Using a pair of tweezers, Janice Tibbals set the tables and put food on the plates. In spite of the size of the job,

> Howard Tibbals gratefully acknowledges the assistance of the many individuals who, "without their enthusiastic help, we would have never been able to set up the model and I feel personally indebted to each for their help."

she revealed that, "I enjoyed it. I got to decide where everybody would sit, as well as what they would be eating. It was like playing with the world's biggest dollhouse." After completing the dining tent, she continued on to the dressing tent where she positioned steamer trunks, mirrors, and makeup – including miniscule tubes of lipstick, combs, brushes, and bars of soap – for each performer on the show.

Just as the big top was the center of the circus experience, the big top was the largest part of the installation. After the tent was laid out, more than five hundred tent stakes were driven into the tabletop and the six main tent poles were raised. Once the top was up, the bleacher seating was installed. From five chair

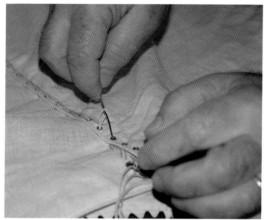

wagons, 7,000 folding chairs were unfolded, and placed on the risers. Equipment for the acts, above, in, and between the three circus rings and on the stages, was rigged and secured. Finally, the acrobats, trainers, animals, dancers, and clowns, were positioned in the rings and the audience placed in their seats: all waiting for the show to begin.

The Circus Museum's Tibbals Learning Center opened in January 2006. For the first time, the entire Howard Bros. Circus Model, complete with eight main tents, 154 wagons, 1,300 circus performers and workers, more than 900 animals, and a 59-car train is on display for the delight of children of all ages.

Howard Tibbals on the
Howard Bros. Circus lot.

THE MAMMOTH MINIATURE CONTINUES TO GROW

When the Howard Bros. Circus Model in the Tibbals Learning Center opened to the public in January 2006, work on the model did not stop for Howard Tibbals; in fact, it still continues today. For Howard, there is always something else that can be added to enhance the model's accuracy. Since 2006, Howard has added five railroad cars to his miniature circus world – two Pullman sleepers, the elephant car that transported Pawah, the white elephant, and no. 1 and no. 3 advertising cars. He has also added two personnel transport vehicles (REO trucks), two additional Mack trucks, two railroad flat cars (no. 101 and no. 102), a bird wagon located in the menagerie tent, a crane truck, wardrobe and bike tents, a ladder for the side show banner, and new elephant and center ring animal acts. As he has done in the past, Howard spent hundreds of hours researching, constructing, painting, and lighting each new addition.

Howard Tibbals is regularly asked what his favorite part of the Howard Bros. Circus Model is; with a smile he replies, "The last piece that I completed!" Another question that Howard is frequently asked is how does he decide on his next project for the model and that question requires a bit more of an explanation. Sometimes, he goes back to his list of things that he feels are still needed to create the most accurate representation of the Ringling Bros. and Barnum & Bailey show. One such project is to complete twenty-six more Pullman sleeping cars. Other times he makes his decision based upon a new photograph that he has acquired. Howard never starts a new project if he does not have all the documentation that is needed to create an accurate model piece. Sometimes, he decides upon a project just because he wants to try his hand at creating something new, like the ladder needed for the side show bannerline, which allows him a break from the more complex projects.

Once he has decided upon a project, Howard Tibbals has an established construction process. First, he pulls together all the information he has on the new project. In the case of the no. 3 advertising railroad car, he will review the Pullman Car Company archives for blueprints, search for documentation, and bring together all the images from his extensive Ringling Bros. and Barnum & Bailey photographic collection. Then with everything at hand, Howard makes a scale drawing and searches for similarities to other projects he has worked on in the past. He also taps other resources such as Harold Dunn's notes on wagons and cars from the winter quarters to verify dimensions. Once the scale drawing is completed, Howard checks out his model building supplies to see if he has all the material needed for the project. For most of his projects, he uses brass rods, piano wire, model airplane plywood, brass round head pins, and, for the larger pieces, he uses Appalachian-hard white maple or solid oak.

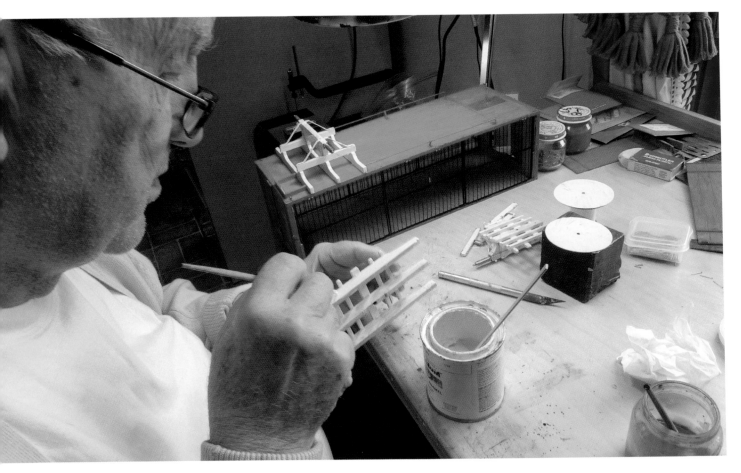

With everything at hand, Howard usually begins work on the most complicated part of the project. This allows him to work out any problems at the beginning rather than at the end of the project. After the construction is completed, all that remains to be done is the painting and lettering of the model piece. However, before Howard starts this final step, he puts the entire model piece together, just to make sure that everything fits correctly. An average wagon takes Howard six to twelve weeks to complete. Because of its complexity, the Frozen Delight wagon took eight months to finish. One of the most difficult undertaking was the side show bannerline. Each of the four wagons took four months to build, paint, and install the lights.

Early on in building the model, Howard Tibbals realized that the model circus was too large for any one individual to complete in a lifetime. Over the years, he has worked with many artists and model builders who have assisted him in carving animals, sculpting people, and building railroad cars and parade wagons. In some cases, Howard provided a prototype of the piece and multiple copies were made from his work. Several of these individuals played a large part in the creation of the model. Harold Dunn became Howard's mentor and helped him to locate photographs and other circus documentation. Their collaboration set a new model-building standard in scope, scale, and detail. Dunn also built a wagon for Howard and

Dunn's wife, Barbara, assisted with painting and sewing the wardrobe. Charlie Deck and Chuck Caldwell helped populate the circus lot with wonderfully-carved animals and sculpted people. Today, individuals like David Duncan and Carolyn and Don McGarvey continue to assist Howard with fulfilling his vision of the most accurate and complete model of The Ringling show under the tent.

But Howard Tibbals also admits that some of the most important individuals never built a single model piece. The presidents, directors, and staff of The Ringling and Florida State University have been critical to the success of the model's installation and interpretation as well as the construction of the Tibbals Learning Center.

Most of all, he is sincerely grateful for the help and expertise of Joseph P. Congleton of Knoxville, Tennessee, and Talbot "Sandy" D'Alemberte, former president of Florida State University, for without their hard work and vision the Howard Bros. Circus Model in the Tibbals Learning Center at The Ringling would have never become a reality.

Some of the model builders and artists who assisted:

- Bill Backstein
- Les Bex
- Charlie Deck
- Barbara and Harold Dunn
- Chuck Caldwell
- David Duncan
- LaNorma Fox
- Joe Kasper
- Robert MacDougall
- Carolyn and Don McGarvey
- George Piercey

Built in ¾" to 1' scale (one-sixteenth lifesize), the Howard Bros. Circus Model boasts some impressive numbers. There are over 42,000 individual pieces in the miniature. The model of a fully grown Asian elephant (left) measures 6⅛ inches tall and weighs 1 pound. In real life the animal would be 8 feet tall and weigh 7,000 pounds!

- 6⅛" is the height of the Giant, the tallest performer (right)
- 2¼" is the height of Daisy Doll, the smallest performer (below)
- 4¼" is the average height of a man in the model
- 5' 2" is the height of a big top center pole with attached flag pole, the tallest piece in the model
- ¼" x ¹⁄₁₆" x ¹⁄₁₆" are the measurements of a nail, the smallest single piece in the model

All individual model pieces are reproduced at actual size except the Red Ticket Wagon on page 38.

Howard Tibbals wrote to the Ringling Bros. and Barnum & Bailey circus in 1956 requesting permission to use the Ringling title on his model railroad and circus wagons, but his request was denied. Tibbals began calling the miniature the Howard Bros. Circus Model and the name stuck. Looking back, Howard Tibbals feels that "they actually saved me a lot of trouble, since I didn't have to put that long, 'Ringling Bros. and Barnum & Bailey Combined Shows' name on everything."

Circus Lingo

- **Back track:** Hippodrome track on the back door side of the big top.
- **Bale ring:** A metal ring, secured to the tent pole by block and tackle, to which the canvas is lashed.
- **Big top:** Main performance tent.
- **Blues:** General admission bleacher seats located at the end of the big top, usually painted blue.
- **Front track:** The hippodrome track facing the grand stand across from the bandstand.
- **Funny ropes:** Extra ropes around the big top at angles to give extra stability to the top.
- **Grandstand:** Seating area nearest the rings.
- **Lacing:** System of eyelets and rope loops that hold together the canvas panels of a tent.
- **Rigging:** Apparatus used in high wire or aerial acts.
- **Ring:** Circle in which circus acts are presented – 42 feet in diameter.
- **Ring curb:** Curved pieces that define the performance area.
- **Spanish web:** A canvas covered rope from which aerialists perform. Web sitters hold the ropes for the act.
- **Straw house:** A sold-out show where bales of straw were used along the hippodrome track for additional seating.

PHOTOGRAPHIC CREDITS

All Howard Bros. Circus Model photography by Jim Stem, Tampa, Florida, except for cover, 2-3, 13, 34, 35, 48, 49, 50, 51, 60, 65, 76-77, inside back cover, by Ron Levere, Sarasota, Florida; inside cover, 46-47, 48, 51, 72, by Claire Smithers, Sarasota, Florida; 73, 74, 75, by Janice Tibbals, Knoxville, Tennessee.

Historic photographs from the Tibbals Collection at The Ringling. Permission to publish the following photographs courtesy of the Circus World Museum, Baraboo, Wisconsin: page 20: Interior of ring stock tent, ca. 1939. Harry A. Atwell; page 30: Lillian Leitzel in her private tent, ca. 1920. Harry A. Atwell; page 35: Sip and Bite wagon, ca. 1920. Harry A. Atwell; page 37: Talker on the midway, ca. 1925. Harry A. Atwell.

Deborah W. Walk, Assistant Director for Legacy and Circus
Jennifer Lemmer Posey, Associate Curator of the Circus Museum
Melissa Porreca McCarriagher, former Tibbals Collection Manager.